P9-CRW-644
3 5674 02435602 5

TOP 10 BASKETBALL LEGENDS

Ken Rappoport

SPORTS TOP 10

ENSLOW PUBLISHERS, INC.

44 Fadem Rd.
Box 699
Springfield, N.J. 07081
U.S.A

P.O. Box 38
Aldershot
Hants GU12 6BP
U.K.

Acknowledgments

The author is most grateful to the following for their contributions to this book: Matthew Siegel and Wayne Patterson at the Naismith Memorial Basketball Hall of Fame, and Pete Steeber of the National Basketball Association media relations department. And, of course, to my wife, Bernice, for her expert editing.

Dedication

For Bernice, As Always

Library of Congress Cataloging-in-Publication Data

Rappoport, Ken.
Top 10 Basketball Legends / Ken Rappoport.
p. cm. — (Sports Top 10)
Includes index.
ISBN 0-89490-610-0
1. Basketball players—United States—Biography—Juvenile literature. I. Title. II. Title: Top ten basketball legends.
III. Series.
GV884.A1R36 1995
796.323'092'2—dc20
[B] 94-32060
CIP
AC

Printed in the United States of America.

10 9 8 7 6 5 4 3 2 1

Photo Credits: Basketball Hall of Fame, pp. 31, 35, 41; DePaul University, p. 33; Focus on Sports, p. 42; Louisiana State University, p. 37; © Mitchell B. Reibel, pp. 6, 9; © Noren Trotman, pp. 10, 13, 18, 21, 22, 25; Robert Crawford, p. 26, 29; Sports Information Office, Holy Cross College, p. 14; Wide World Photos, Inc., pp. 17, 39, 45.

Cover Photo: Robert Crawford

Interior Design: Richard Stalzer

CONTENTS

Javon Kellogg 48

Introduction

What Is A Basketball Genius? A player who is so good that he or she raises the awareness of the playing position. The players in this book can be considered such creative talents.

Wilt Chamberlain, Kareem Abdul-Jabbar, and Bill Russell are usually included when listing all-time greats. I have decided to write about some deserving alternates for the starting lineup of "Top 10 Basketball Legends."

Before "Wilt the Stilt," Jabbar, and Russell, there was George Mikan. Mikan showed that a center needn't be just a big immovable object under the basket. Mikan could pass, shoot, rebound, and move with the skill of a smaller player.

Bob Pettit brought a new dimension to the game with his trend-setting jump shot that made him the first of the high-scoring forwards. He was also a brilliant rebounder who used intelligent positioning rather than sheer strength to outfox bigger players.

Rick Barry was the first of the great passing forwards and the best foul shooter in National Basketball Association (NBA) history. Julius Erving made theater out of the dunk shot. And although Larry Bird was neither the biggest, strongest, nor quickest—he could dominate basketball with his intense competitiveness and instinctive "sixth-sense" skills.

At the guard position, Bob Cousy was a ballhandling magician. His behind-the-back passes bedeviled opponents of the Boston Celtics. Oscar Robertson was a combination of three players in one—a shooting guard, a playmaking guard, and a small forward. Jerry West was known as "Mr. Clutch." He had an uncanny ability to perform at his best when the game was on the line. Magic Johnson made big guards fashionable in the NBA. He was a basketball chameleon, adjusting his game to any situation. Michael Jordan literally took the position of guard to a higher level with his gravity-defying flights to the basket. He was basketball's greatest player and greatest attraction at the time of his stunning retirement announcement in 1993. You might have other players in mind. Here are my choices.

Career Statistics

Player	NBA Seasons	Games	FG%	Rebounds	FT%	Assists	Points	Average
RICK BARRY	10	794	.449	5,168	.900	4,017	18,395	23.2
LARRY BIRD	13	897	.496	8,974	.886	5,695	21,791	24.3
BOB COUSY	14	924	.375	4,786	.803	6,955	16,960	18.4
JULIUS ERVING	11	836	.507	5,601	.777	3,224	18,364	22.0
MAGIC JOHNSON	12	874	.521	6,376	.848	9,921	17,239	19.7
MICHAEL JORDAN	9	667	.516	4,219	.846	3,935	21,541	32.3
GEORGE MIKAN	9	520	.404	4,167	.778	1,245	11,764	22.6
BOB PETTIT	11	792	.432	12,849	.761	2,369	20,880	26.4
OSCAR ROBERTSON	14	1,040	.485	7,804	.838	9,887	26,710	25.7
JERRY WEST	14	932	.474	5,376	.814	6,238	25,192	27.0

RICK BARRY

Rick Barry played hard in pursuit of the perfect game. Unfortunately, he often lost his cool with his teammates and other players as well.

Rick Barry

Rick Barry Looked Like a movie star with his long blond hair and confident air. Barry was a celebrated, controversial, six-foot seven-inch forward with the San Francisco Warriors.

Basketball seemed like child's play to Barry. And he made the game look easy—scoring with driving twisting layups, with running hook shots from either hand, or with jump shots from as far away as 30 feet.[1]

He stunned the opposition with his speed. Barry did everything quickly—from driving fast cars to driving the lane. "Speed is what I like about basketball," Barry said.[2]

Barry craved action. He had a fierce intensity and a competitive nature, both on and off the court. He had to be Number 1 in everything—even first into the showers after practice. If he wasn't first, he sulked like a child.[3]

Barry wanted his game to be perfect, and he expected perfection from everyone. His reactions were instantaneous and sometimes cruel. When he lost his cool, he screamed at teammates for their mistakes.

As the top player at Roselle High School in New Jersey, Barry received many offers from colleges. He chose the University of Miami because he admired coach Bruce Hale. Hale tried to help Barry control his temper.

As a senior, Barry led the nation in scoring. Even though he was a unanimous All-American, Barry's professional career was in doubt. The pro teams saw him as too thin, too emotional, and too selfish.

Barry was the first pick by the San Francisco Warriors in the 1965 National Basketball Association (NBA) draft. He became the fourth rookie in NBA history to score over 2,000 points. He was also voted the league's Rookie of the Year.

Early in his career Barry faced the Cincinnati Royals and the great Oscar Robertson, another perfectionist. With about two minutes left, Robertson sank a foul shot to give the Royals a 107–106 lead over the Warriors. Barry responded. He dribbled hard across the key, went up high, and hit a spinning jump shot. With 25 seconds in the game, the Warriors led, 109–107. Then Robertson's basket tied the game at 109.

Overtime—Barry's time to outdo himself, to be Number 1. In the first minute, he drove outside the key, dribbled to his right, then went up for a basket. Twisting, he sunk a lefthanded hook. The Warriors took the lead, and Barry became hot. With one minute to go, Barry grabbed his own rebound and reshot the ball. He was fouled on the score.

Sending Rick Barry to the free throw line was like putting money in the bank. He was the greatest free-throw shooter in NBA history. His dad, a former semi-pro player and coach, taught Barry a trick. Barry's dad taught him to shoot underhanded foul shots for better accuracy. At the foul line, as usual, Barry completed the three-point play. He helped the Warriors win, 123–120.[4]

Barry became the only player in basketball history to win scoring titles in college and in two professional leagues—the NBA and the American Basketball Association (ABA).

After playing in the ABA, Barry returned to the NBA. He had his best season in 1974–1975. Barry was mostly responsible for the Warriors' first NBA championship. He averaged 30.6 points, led the NBA in steals, and was the only forward in the top ten in assists.

Barry's career ended in Houston, Texas. His message to kids today: "There's nothing wrong with playing the way Rick Barry played, but don't act the way Rick Barry acted."[5]

Rick Barry

BORN: March 28, 1944, Elizabeth, New Jersey.

HIGH SCHOOL: Roselle High School, Roselle, New Jersey.

COLLEGE: University of Miami (Fla.), 1961–1965.

PRO: San Francisco Warriors, 1965–1967; Oakland Oaks (ABA), 1968–1969; Washington Capitols (ABA), 1969–1970; New York Nets (ABA), 1970–1972; Golden State Warriors, 1972–1978; Houston Rockets, 1978–1980.

RECORDS: Led the NBA in steals, Only NBA forward in the top ten in assists.

HONORS: Basketball Hall of Fame.

Barry's passion for winning included a high-speed style of play on the basketball court and fast cars.

Larry Bird is hard at work on the court earning an honest day's pay.

Larry Bird

Larry Bird Was Determined. His teammates could see it in his eyes as he put on his green and white Boston Celtic uniform. Was he still angry? Bird had blasted his teammates the day before. He called them "a bunch of sissies" when they lost to Los Angeles in Game 3 of the 1984 National Basketball Association (NBA) finals. Bird had to shake up the Celtics. Another loss and the Celtics would be one game from elimination.

The referee tossed the ball for the opening tip-off. Smack! The ball flew into open court, players scrambled for it. Bird flung himself head first into the sweaty, straining tangle of bodies. He stretched his six-foot nine-inch frame to its limit. Firmly gripping the ball, Bird tied up a Laker player. The referee called a jump ball.

The Celtics went on to an overtime victory that night. Eventually, Boston won the NBA championship.[1] But that one moment—diving recklessly for a ball at the tip-off—symbolized Bird's thirteen-year NBA career. He never played a game unless it was nonstop and all-out from start to finish.

Bird often turned tragedy, like his father's suicide, to triumph. He worked hard and became a basketball star at Springs Valley High School in French Lick, Indiana. His next stop: University of Indiana. But Bird left without playing a game. People called him a quitter. Then Bird enrolled at nearby Northwood Institute. He left. "Quitter!" Giving up on school and basketball, he drove a garbage truck. He married, fathered a child, and then divorced his wife. At one of the lowest points of Bird's life, the Indiana State basketball coach convinced him to give college one more try.

In the 1978–79 season, Bird led the Sycamores to the

No. 1 ranking, a 33-game winning streak, and the National Collegiate Athletic Association (NCAA) finals. In the finals, Magic Johnson's Michigan State team beat the Sycamores. Bird, however, was college player of the year.

Bird came to Boston with a five-year $3.25 million contract—the highest at that time for a rookie in the NBA. The Celtics were no longer the dominant team in the NBA. But Bird made an immediate impact. The Celtics were restored to glory.

Bird was the best passing forward of his time—the most complete player. Passing, shooting, rebounding, defense—Bird did all these well. But Bird's best talent was more mental than physical. He had an ability to "read" the game, a sixth sense that let him see plays before others could.[2]

Rewards came in threes for Bird—three NBA championships and three Most Valuable Player (MVP) awards. He was master of the three-point shot. At the NBA All-Star Game, Bird won the long-distance shooting three times.

In the 1988 play-offs, the Celtics were clinging to an 84–82 lead over the Atlanta Hawks at the end of three quarters. They were playing in the seventh and final game of the Eastern Conference finals. Then Bird put on a one-man show. He started the final quarter with 16-foot and 13-foot jumpers from the right side. Then, stealing the ball, he scored off a baseline drive for another basket.

Next he hit a lefthanded jumper in the lane, and then a 17-footer—once again from the right side. With 1:43 remaining he hit a three-pointer from the left side. Then with 26 seconds left he scored with a driving lefthanded layup. The Celtics now led, 114–109. Finally Bird passed to a teammate at midcourt to set up another basket. Bird finished with 20 points in the fourth quarter—34 overall. The Celtics won, 118—116.[3]

"I always know what's happening on the court," Bird said. "I know exactly what I can and cannot do."[4]

Larry Bird

BORN: December 7, 1956, West Baden, Indiana.

HIGH SCHOOL: Springs Valley, French Lick, Indiana.

COLLEGE: Indiana State University, Terre Haute, Ind., 1975–1979.

PRO: Boston Celtics, 1979–1992.

RECORDS: Career Record for Most Offensive Rebounds in Playoffs.

HONORS: Twelve-time all star; Member of 1992 Olympic Gold-Medal Winning Dream Team; Rookie of the Year in his first season; Three-time MVP; Three-time winner of the 3-point competition; Two-time NBA Finals MVP.

Bird's talent was as much mental as it was physical. He had an ability to "read" the game that let him see plays taking shape before others on the court could.

BOB COUSY

Bob Cousy, the "Cooz", created a style of play for generations to come.

Bob Cousy

Bob Cousy Had The Ball near midcourt for Holy Cross College. Trapped, he tried to dribble to his right. Loyola of Chicago defenders were in his face. He had no room.

Suddenly, Cousy's imagination took flight. Instinctively he switched the ball from his right to left hand and dribbled behind his back. He then cut to his left. Dribbling toward the basket, Cousy banked a lefthanded hook shot off the glass backboard and through the net. Holy Cross won![1]

Cousy made razzle-dazzle plays an everyday occurrence. In the pros, he was the creative force that led the Boston Celtics to six NBA championships.

As a young boy, Cousy always showed a courageous spirit. Thirteen-year-old Bob Cousy was nearly at the top of the tree when his foot slipped. Grabbing onto a branch, he tried to regain his balance. Unable to support his weight, the branch snapped. Cousy crashed onto the sidewalk. Agonizing pain seared his right arm. The shooting arm was broken.[2] How would he play basketball? Bob Cousy found a way. He continued to play—lefthanded.

Cousy was with hundreds of hopefuls when he tried out for the high school basketball team. Because of his average height, the coach didn't notice him. Later he saw Cousy in a gym hitting shots lefthanded. "Why don't you come out for the team?" the coach asked. "I need a lefthander for my system."[3] As a fifteen-year-old Cousy was an average high school player. Then he made himself a promise to become an All-American. While other kids in his Queens, New York, neighborhood went to the movies on Saturday afternoons, Cousy practiced basketball. Success followed: All-Scholastic in high school. Then All-American in college.

When Cousy joined the pros, the NBA only had one superstar—George Mikan. It also had a slow-footed style of play. Cousy speeded up the game with his dazzling passes and magic playmaking. Cousy popularized the behind-the-back and between-the-legs dribble and the "no-look" pass. Cousy's "twice-around pass" also thrilled fans. Thanks to that childhood accident, Cousy could switch the ball between hands while going up for a shot and shoot lefthanded or righthanded. In the 1950s Cousy was a point guard (specializing in passing and playmaking) years before the position had a name.

But before Cousy changed the game, he had to change Red Auerbach's mind. The general manager of the Boston Celtics passed over Cousy in the college draft. Too flashy, he thought. When another team folded, Cousy wound up with the Celtics anyway.[4]

Cousy led the NBA for eight straight seasons in assists. He was often the Celtics' high scorer as well during his thirteen-year career. The night of March 21, 1953, the Celtics were on the verge of a team first. The team was playing the Syracuse Nationals in the first round of playoffs. Cousy, playing on a bad leg, scored only 7 points in the first half. He scored 18 in the second, sinking a foul shot that sent the game into overtime, tied at 77.

In the first overtime Cousy scored 6 of Boston's points. This included a foul shot that again tied the game in the final seconds. In the second overtime Cousy scored all 4 points for the Celtics. Again the score was tied. Cousy scored 8 points in the third overtime. His 25-foot jumper tied the game at 99 in the closing seconds. A fourth overtime was needed. This time the Nationals jumped out to a 104–99 lead. Then Cousy scored 5 straight points to tie the game. Boston finally pulled out the game, 111–105. The six-foot one-inch Cousy created a style of play for future generations to follow.

Bob Cousy

Born: August 9, 1928, New York, N.Y.
High School: Andrew Jackson, Queens, N.Y.
College: Holy Cross College, Worcester, MA, 1946–1950.
Pro: Boston Celtics, 1950–1963; Cincinnati Royals, 1969–1970.
Records: Led the NBA for 8 straight seasons in assists.
Honors: NBA MVP, 1 year; NBA All-star, every year.

Bob Cousy's exciting style of play—switching the ball from his right hand to his left while going up for a shot, dribbling behind his back, and fancy moves on the court—made the game of basketball a lot of fun for fans to watch.

JULIUS ERVING

Julius Erving took the basketball that kids play on the playground and refined and fine-tuned it.

Julius Erving

It Was The 1980 NBA finals. Julius Erving, playing for the Philadelphia 76ers, took a step and dribbled around the Los Angeles Lakers' Mark Landsberger. Rocket-like, the six-foot six-inch Erving launched himself toward the basket.[1]

However, there was a tall obstacle in his way—Kareem Abdul-Jabbar. The seven-foot two-inch Laker center had his arms stretched skyward, blocking Erving's path. But Erving found another way.

Gliding to his left in mid-air, Erving was now beyond the backboard. He brought the ball down in his right hand, reached out, and softly flipped the ball off the backboard and into the basket. He had completed an underhand reverse-scoop layup for two points! Erving had floated through the air and landed like a cat on the court. The spectacular play recalled his early days in the former American Basketball Association (ABA). There he routinely performed such razzle-dazzle moves on a daily basis.

It was these types of plays early in his career that earned Erving a nickname—"the Doctor." Later in the pros this was shortened to "Dr. J." Erving's movement to the basket could be compared to a surgeon's skill—a steady hand knifing through opposing defenses.

After his father left the family and his younger brother Michael died at the age of sixteen, Erving became tougher and more self-confident. Determined to escape from his surroundings, he set goals for himself.

Erving was able to do things with a basketball that no one had ever seen before. He was a forward who handled the ball like a guard. And he took the game to another level with his creative dunk shots.

Dribbling at full speed to the foul line, Erving would stop and go airborne twenty feet from the basket. Flying through the air, he would dunk the ball through the hoop as if it were shot by a gun. It was the "Foul-Line Takeoff Tomahawk."

Erving, one of only three players to score 30,000 points as of the 1994–1995 season, was Most Valuable Player (MVP) four times in his sixteen-year career in the ABA and NBA. He was also an All-Star MVP twice while appearing in sixteen All-Star Games. Erving was selected to the NBA's 35th anniversary team and inducted into the Basketball Hall of Fame.

Erving led his teams to three championships, two of them in the ABA. In the 1983 NBA finals, Erving found himself facing the Lakers again. This time the 76ers were holding a 3–0 advantage in the best-of-seven series. But the 76ers trailed in Game 4 by 11 points in the fourth quarter.

Philadelphia narrowed the lead, and then Erving took command. With 2:02 remaining he flicked the ball away from Jabbar, raced downcourt, and dunked it. With 59 seconds left Erving scored on a driving three-point play. Then with 24 seconds remaining, he floated in a jumper from the top of the key. The final score: Philadelphia, 115; Los Angeles, 108. Erving had led the 76ers to a sweep of a great Laker team!

"The playground game refined," was the way Erving described his style.[2]

JULIUS ERVING

BORN: February 22, 1950, Roosevelt, New York.

HIGH SCHOOL: Roosevelt High School, Roosevelt, New York.

COLLEGE: University of Massachusetts, Amherst, MA, 1968–1971.

PRO: Virginia Squires (ABA), 1971–1973; New York Nets (ABA), 1973–1976; Philadelphia 76ers, 1976–1987.

HONORS: NBA MVP, 1981; Elected to Naismith Memorial Basketball Hall of Fame, 1993.

Erving was able to do things with a basketball that no one had ever seen before. "Dr. J" was a smooth operator.

Magic Johnson gets by his defender and the fans are treated to another "Showtime" in Los Angeles.

Magic Johnson

The Spotlight Was On Magic Johnson at center court. He was playing in Game 6 of the 1980 NBA finals between the Los Angeles Lakers and Philadelphia 76ers. The Lakers were one game away from the NBA championship.

Kareem Abdul-Jabbar, the Lakers' All-Star center and best player, was out with a sprained ankle. As a last-minute replacement, Johnson was going to take the tipoff. It was a desperate move by the Lakers. They were the underdogs without Jabbar.

The center position was completely new to Magic Johnson. Normally Johnson played guard.

As Magic Johnson trotted out to center court, he recalled the thrill of sitting in Jabbar's seat on the team flight. He was ready for the challenge. Johnson faced Caldwell Jones, the 76ers' seven-foot center who was three inches taller.

But Johnson didn't take long to feel at home in the center position as well at any other position on the court! Switching between center, point guard, shooting guard, power forward, and small forward, Johnson played all *five* positions.

The Lakers beat the 76ers, 123–107, in Game 6. This win gave the team its first world championship since 1972.[1]

The Lakers became the team of the 1980s in the NBA. With eight conference titles and five NBA championships, Magic Johnson was their man.

Winning championships had become a way of life for Johnson. At Everett High School in Lansing, Michigan, he led his team to the state championship in his senior year.[2] In those years he was Earvin Johnson. Then a reporter nicknamed him "Magic." Johnson's mother feared the nickname set unrealistic standards.[3] But Magic Johnson managed to live up to the standards.

As a college sophomore in 1979, he led Michigan State to the national championship. Johnson outplayed Indiana State's Larry Bird in the title game.

At six-feet nine-inches, Johnson was the tallest guard in the NBA. Tall players are not known for their ballhandling skills. But few handled the ball better than Johnson.

Johnson's skills, big smile, and enthusiasm brought the Lakers back to life. They became his team. Magic Johnson had the Hollywood dream: a $25 million contract, fame, and fans who loved him. Then, suddenly, the dream turned into a nightmare.

In 1981 the Lakers' coach was fired and Johnson, who had disagreed with the coach's strategy, was blamed. Every time Johnson picked up the ball, he was booed.

In 1984 the Lakers lost the NBA championship to Boston and Magic's arch-rival, Larry Bird. Again Johnson was blamed. "When you miss the shots, you go home and you sit in the dark," he said.[4] But Johnson was shocked by the negative reaction of the media that had once loved him.

Magic Johnson was doubly determined to be a winner again. And in 1985 he helped restore the Lakers to the top of the NBA. The team won its third championship in six years.

Johnson was the NBA's Most Valuable Player (MVP) three times and was in the prime of his career when the announcement came. Doctors found the HIV virus in his blood. The HIV virus leads to the deadly disease AIDS. The news shocked the world and forced an emotional Magic Johnson to retire early from his beloved sport.

One last moment of glory lay ahead: the 1992 Olympics in Barcelona, Spain. At the opening day ceremonies, Johnson stole the show. In an emotional outburst, everyone reached out to him. In a happy ending, his "Dream Team" brought home the Gold Medal.

Magic Johnson

Born: August 15, 1959, Lansing, Michigan.

High School: Everett High School, Lansing, MI.

College: Michigan State, East Lansing, MI, 1977–1979.

Pro: Los Angeles Lakers, 1979–1992.

Records: Most assists in a career and highest assists per-game average.

Honors: NBA MVP, three times; Member of 1992 Olympic Gold-Medal Dream Team.

Part of Magic Johnson's mystique on the court is his unique ability to use his crafty hand moves to beat his opponents.

MICHAEL JORDAN

Michael Jordan brought excitement to the city of Chicago and to the National Basketball Association with his dazzling style of play.

Michael Jordan

It Was A Winning Season. It was a tragic year. The basketball world stood waiting. Michael Jordan would make the most important decision of his life. After nine years of success both on and off the basketball court, Jordan was considering the big "R"—retirement. Why?[1]

Jordan, considered the best basketball player in the world, had just led the Chicago Bulls to their third straight National Basketball Association (NBA) championship. The league scoring title was his for the seventh straight year. As an international celebrity, Jordan had it all: fame and fortune. At thirty, he was in the prime of his career. Why retire?

Had his career become too hard on him? Too much success too soon? Jordan did lead a goldfish-bowl type of existence. Recently, disputes with the media, negative publicity, and suffocating fans seemed to be daily events. And then there was the murder.

Michael Jordan's father had been missing. His red $40,000 sports car was found abandoned. The Jordan family and Jordan's fans waited anxiously.

On August 3, 1993, James Jordan's body was found in a South Carolina creek. He had been shot. James Jordan had been an important force in his son's life. Now Michael Jordan grieved for his friend and adviser.

Jordan's amazing basketball career didn't begin until college. He became a hero in the 1982 National Collegiate Athletic Association (NCAA) playoffs. The North Carolina Tar Heels were one game away from winning the national championship.

The Georgetown Hoyas led, 32–31, at halftime. The second

half was equally close. With 32 seconds left, Georgetown led, 62–61.

There were only 17 seconds remaining when Jordan, a cool, confident, freshman guard, fired in a 17-foot jump shot. The national championship now belonged to the Tar Heels for the first time since 1957. Jordan was an instant folk hero.[2]

Next came the Chicago Bulls. The Bulls had been a mediocre franchise. Jordan made an immediate impact on the Bulls in 1984. Watching his acrobatic brilliance, a thrill surged through the crowd. What would he do next? Opponents weren't sure what he would do either.

Jordan's athletic ability was amazing: incredible dunks over players nearly a foot taller; knifing between bewildered defenders like a shadow; switching the ball from one hand to the other while soaring over players toward the basket; double-clutching in mid-air before making mind-boggling shots; and creating space for his jump shot where none seemed to exist.[3]

A broken bone in his left foot sidelined Jordan for most of the 1985–1986 season. Then he returned with a vengeance in the 1986 playoff series against Boston. He scored 49 points and then a record 63 against the Celtics.

In the 1991 finals against the Los Angeles Lakers, Jordan made his signature shot. Jordan drove to the basket, soared into the air over the heads of his opponents, hung in the air, switched the ball from his right to his left hand, and dropped the ball through the basket.

But Jordan's biggest shot was yet to be fired. The Bulls called a news conference on October 6, 1993. Reporters and television crews flooded the Bulls' training facility. Now the media listened. Jordan was retiring. "I just feel that I don't have anything else to prove. The desire just isn't there."[4]

Even with early retirement, Jordan had left a legacy for the ages.

MICHAEL JORDAN

BORN: February 17, 1963, Brooklyn, New York.

HIGH SCHOOL: Emsley A. Laney, Wilmington, N.C.

COLLEGE: University of North Carolina, Chapel Hill, N.C., 1981–1984.

PRO: Chicago Bulls, 1984-1993.

RECORDS: Led Bulls to three straight NBA championships; Highest career points-per-game average.

HONORS: Three times NBA Most Valuable Player; NBA Rookie of the Year; Six times All-NBA First Team; Once all-NBA Second Team, Five times All-NBA Defensive First Team.

Even early on during his college days at North Carolina, Jordan shows his dunking ability.

GEORGE MIKAN

"SHOOT, MIKE, SHOOT!" "Mike" was George Mikan, the star center for the DePaul Blue Demons and the glamour player of college basketball. On this April night in 1945, a sellout crowd filled New York's Madison Square Garden for the semifinals of the National Invitation Tournament (NIT).

Mikan just kept scoring. When the totals were in, he had an amazing 53 points—as many as the entire Rhode Island team! The final score was DePaul, 97; Rhode Island, 53.[1]

Mikan was different. Because of his height, he was regarded as a freak. In the 1930s people were shorter than today. At age eight, Mikan was five-feet nine-inches, and at eleven, he reached six feet.[2] At six-foot ten-inches and 245 pounds, Mikan was a big man, bigger yet for his time.

"Frankenstein!" "Monster!" The teasing rang in his ears all through his youth. Why did he have to be so big? There was no place that Mikan felt comfortable—not even on a basketball court. He tried out for the high school basketball team. But poor eyesight forced him to wear glasses. "I don't like players who have to wear glasses...turn in your suit," the coach snapped.[3]

Rejected, Mikan decided to become a priest. After Mikan enrolled at Quigley Preparatory Seminary in Chicago, a priest advised him, "The priesthood is no place for anybody who's trying to run away."

Mikan decided to give basketball another try. His height was enough to attract attention. At Notre Dame the coach said, "Hopelessly clumsy." Rejected again.

The Notre Dame assistant coach Ray Meyer gave the youngster some encouragement. "Don't worry, kid, you'll be

GEORGE MIKAN

George Mikan was exceptionally large for his time, and he wore glasses. He overcame his awkwardness to become a great basketball player.

a basketball player somewhere else." "Somewhere else" turned out to be DePaul. Meyer became the DePaul coach, and Mikan made the team. To overcome Mikan's clumsiness, Meyer put him through a series of difficult workouts.

Mikan went on to win All-America honors and was twice named college Player of the Year. Mikan brought DePaul a national basketball championship in the NIT.

In the 1940s, college basketball was far more popular than the pros. When Mikan turned professional in 1946, the National Basketball Association (NBA) had not been established. Big athletic basketball players such as seven-foot, 300-pound Shaquille O'Neal didn't exist.

Mikan was a rarity in basketball in his time—a big man who could shoot, rebound, and pass. When Mikan played, the game was slower than it is today. The fast-break style of basketball was unknown. The 24-second shot clock didn't exist, and teams held the ball as long as they wanted.

In one game against Mikan's Minneapolis Lakers, the Fort Wayne Pistons held the ball nearly the entire night and won, 19–18. This score was the lowest in NBA history. The "slow-down game" forced the NBA to go to the 24-second clock.[4] Mikan positioned himself under the basket and no one could move him. Mostly because of Mikan, the NBA changed its rule book. The league widened the lane from six to twelve feet, and made it illegal for a player to stay longer than three seconds in the lane.[5]

But the rules didn't stop Mikan. He simply adjusted his game. As record after record was broken, he established himself as the biggest force in basketball with the powerful Minneapolis Lakers—pro basketball's first dynasty. The Lakers won championships in three different leagues.

In an Associated Press poll, he was voted the "Greatest Basketball Player of the First Half-Century." Mikan had learned to overcome the "disadvantage" of height and stand tall.

George Mikan

Born: June 18, 1924, Joliet, Illinois.

High School: Joliet Catholic, Quigley Prep, Chicago, IL.

College: DePaul University, Chicago, IL, 1941–1946.

Pro: Chicago Stags (NBL), 1946–1947; Minneapolis Lakers (NBL, BAA, NBA) 1947–1956.

Honors: Twice named College Player of the Year; Helped Lakers to win three different championships in three different leagues; Voted Greatest Basketball Player of the First Half-Century; Basketball Hall of Fame; five times All-NBA First Team.

By the time George Mikan was eleven years old, he had already reached six feet in height.

Bob Pettit

He Came Onto The Court wearing a heavy white cast on his left hand. Bob Pettit was ready to play in the 1958 National Basketball Association (NBA) All-Star Game. The St. Louis Hawks' star faced the game's greatest defensive center—Bill Russell of the Boston Celtics. How could a player with a broken hand battle superstars under the basket?

Pettit answered with a display of agility and courage. During a confrontation with Russell, Pettit twice had his jump shots batted down. Despite wearing the cast, Pettit was still able to beat Russell to the ball.

On his third try, Pettit faked out the Boston great with a twist. He went up for a basket as the home crowd at the St. Louis Arena screamed with delight. That score was just 2 of an All-Star record 28 points in the game. Pettit, amazingly, also pulled down 26 rebounds. He would later break this rebounding record in the 1962 All-Star Game.[1]

As an awkward teenager, Pettit didn't show the slightest sign of athletic ability. When he was cut from the football, baseball, and basketball teams at Baton Rouge (Louisiana) High School, his confidence was at an all-time low. Hoping to boost his son's confidence, his father put up a basket in the backyard. Pettit shot baskets for hours.

By his senior year Pettit had improved enough to help his team win the state championship. Quite an accomplishment for a player who had been rejected only a few years before!

Just two weeks before his first pro season, Pettit was given a seemingly impossible task. He was to learn the forward position. He had been a center throughout his high school and college career. Could he do it? He wasn't sure.

Bob Pettit went from being an awkward teenager to the key player of the St. Louis Hawks.

"The whole thing was like telling a rookie catcher he had to win a job at shortstop to stay in the big leagues," Pettit recalled. "For two months I was a feeble imitation of a No. 1 draft choice. I was sucked out of position by simple feints, sometimes twice on the same play."[2] But Pettit and a handful of others established a new shooting style.

By the midpoint of the 1954–1955 season, Pettit finally arrived and won the Rookie of the Year award. It was a personal triumph.

In 1958 the Hawks were playing the Boston Celtics in the deciding game of the NBA championship. Pettit was on a roll, scoring 31 points through the first three quarters.

If not for Pettit, the Hawks would have been "dead birds." As it was, the team was pushing the powerful Celtics to the limit. A surge put the Celtics ahead early in the fourth quarter. Then back came the Hawks to tie the see-saw game. Now there was only 6:16 to go. Pettit scored to give St. Louis a 95–93 lead.

Three times the Celtics battled back within a point. But each time Pettit sank a basket that kept his team in front.

Pettit's last basket, and 50th point, gave the Hawks their winning margin. The Hawks beat the Celtics, 110–109, for their first NBA championship.

Pettit had a remarkable "nose" for rebounds. He knew where to position himself so he could outrebound taller and heavier opponents. Offensive rebounds were Pettit's specialty. Pettit followed his shots aggressively.

Pettit was in the top five among rebounders in each of his eleven seasons except his last, when he was injured. At the end of his career he ranked No. 3 on the NBA's all-time rebounding list.

Pettit was the NBA's Most Valuable Player (MVP) twice, a first-team forward ten years in a row, an All-Star ten straight years, and a winner of the All-Star MVP trophy four times.

Bob Pettit

BORN: December 12, 1932, Baton Rouge, Louisiana.

HIGH SCHOOL: Baton Rouge High School, Baton Rouge, Louisiana.

COLLEGE: Louisiana State, Baton Rouge, LA, 1950–1954.

PRO: Milwaukee Hawks, 1954–1955; St. Louis Hawks, 1955–1965.

RECORDS: Two-time MVP; No. 3 in NBA all-time rebounding.

HONORS: Rookie of the Year, 1954-1955; All-Star 10 straight years.

Pettit had a knack for getting rebounds. He knew where to position himself so that he could outrebound taller and heavier opponents.

Oscar Robertson

Cincinnati Versus Seton Hall: at center court was Oscar Robertson. With a 30-point scoring average, he was the new hotshot in college basketball. In fact, the University of Cincinnati star was the most talked-about player during the 1957–1958 season. Could a nineteen-year-old sophomore stand the pressure of playing at Madison Square Garden?

Thirty-five seconds into the game against Seton Hall, Robertson's nervousness was apparent. He drove the lane for a layup, floated into the air, but missed an easy basket.

Robertson's performance seemed to be a classic case of Garden jitters. However, his slump didn't last long. About a minute later Robertson spun and sank an underhanded layup. Then he started to click. Stretching out his long arms, the six-foot five-inch Robertson fired in jump shots with either hand, hook shots from the foul line, drives, and tap-ins. He also passed to teammates, grabbed rebounds, and intercepted passes.

When Robertson was finished, he had scored 56 points—a Garden record—and set three other basketball records. Robertson's Bearcats thrashed Seton Hall, 118–54. "This is the greatest sophomore I've ever seen," St. John's coach Joe Lapchick said.[1]

In the pros, Robertson became the king of the "triple-double." What is a triple-double? It is scored whenever a player reaches double figures in three categories in a game—usually points, rebounds, and assists.

To pull off a triple-double in one game is a great accomplishment. Robertson just about averaged a triple-double for seven years! With the Cincinnati Royals, he averaged 30.4

OSCAR ROBERTSON

As a young boy, Oscar Robertson vowed to be a good basketball player so that his older brothers would let him play in their games.

points, 10.7 assists, and 9.4 rebounds a game in his first seven years in the National Basketball Association (NBA).[2]

Robertson was the game's first "super" guard. He was a point guard who directed the offense, a shooting guard who scored amazing point totals, and a fierce rebounder who could match most of the NBA's forwards. Robertson was also a master of the three-point play—scoring a basket and drawing a foul. Opponents feared guarding Robertson.

But Robertson was not always a good player. As a young boy in Indianapolis, he discovered basketball at the local YMCA. Being the youngest in the family is often difficult. Robertson was often excluded from his older brothers' games. He vowed to make himself a good player "so they'd have to let me play."

Robertson's favorite hangout was the "Dust Bowl." This was a vacant lot a few blocks from his house. There the local kids got together for pickup games.

At Crispus Attucks High School in Indianapolis, Robertson led his team to a 45-game winning streak and two straight state championships. It was the first state championship won by an all-black school in Indiana. Robertson then went to the University of Cincinnati, where he led the nation in scoring for three seasons and was twice named Player of the Year.

Robertson was a proud man and he resented the way African Americans were treated. In college and the pros, he stood up for his rights—both on and off the court. He battled with management over contracts and set the precedent for today's player salaries.

Robertson was NBA Rookie of the Year in 1961, league Most Valuable Player (MVP) in 1964, and twelve-time All-Star.

Robertson realized a dream when he played on the U.S. basketball team at the 1960 Olympics. The team won the Gold Medal. But it was eleven years before Robertson could realize another dream—an NBA championship.

Oscar Robertson

Born: November 24, 1938, Charlotte, Tennessee.
High School: Crispus Attucks High School, Indianapolis, Indiana.
College: University of Cincinnati, Cincinnati, OH, 1956–1960.
Pro: Cincinnati Royals, 1960–1970; Milwaukee Bucks,1970–1973.
Records: Averaged nearly Triple-doubles for seven years.
Honors: NBA Rookie of the Year, 1961; League MVP, 1969; Twelve-time All Star.

Oscar Robertson was the game's first "super" guard. He directed the offense, scored incredible point totals, and was a tough rebounder.

JERRY WEST

Jerry West was known as "Mr. Clutch" for his remarkable ability to make shots when it counted.

Jerry West

Time Was Running Out On the Los Angeles Lakers. The team was two points down to the New York Knicks. Only seconds were left in the 1970 National Basketball Association (NBA) play-offs.

Jerry West had the ball behind the half-court line, about 60 feet from the basket. West's teammates were well guarded, and there was no time to bring the ball upcourt to set up a play. Only a miracle could save the Lakers.

West took the shot. The ball sailed across the court and swished through the net as time ran out! The game was tied.

The Knicks' Dave Debusschere sank to his knees. The Lakers' center Wilt Chamberlain, thinking the shot had ended the game, rushed off the court. He wasn't the only one who was confused.

The excited Lakers' announcer called West's shot an "80-footer." It wasn't quite that, but it was one of the most memorable shots ever made in the NBA play-offs.

The Lakers eventually lost to the Knicks, but West's incredible shot at the end of regulation time stamped him as one of the great clutch players in the game.[1]

At West Virginia University, West was nicknamed "Tarantula" because his unusually long arms helped him snatch rebounds and steal passes from frustrated opponents.

West was also courageous. Against Kentucky in the 1959 National Collegiate Athletic Association (NCAA) tournament, his nose was broken during the first half. But West refused to leave the game.

At halftime in the dressing room, the trainer stuffed gauze in West's nose to keep it from bleeding. Gulping air through his mouth, he helped his team upset the Wildcats, 79–70.[2]

West was about average size for a backcourt player in the NBA. But that was the only trait that was average about him. He had one of the quickest shots. West found if he pounded his last dribble with more force, it gave him a quicker release. A natural righthander, as a youth in Cheylan, West Virginia, he taught himself to dribble lefthanded.

In 1962 the Lakers played the Boston Celtics for the NBA Championship. The score was tied with 3 seconds left. Boston attempted to inbound the ball at midcourt. But West intercepted the pass, dribbled quickly toward the basket, and scored. The Celtics thought this was impossible. No one could steal the ball, dribble half the length of the court, and score in just three seconds. The instant replay showed that the Celtics were wrong. West had used up just 2.7 seconds![3]

When he retired after 14 years in the NBA, West's scoring average of 27 points a game was the fifth highest in basketball history. His performances in the play-offs were also remarkable. He averaged 29.1 points, and when he retired, West was the all-time leading scorer in play-off history.

Unofficially he also led the NBA in broken noses—nine. Blame it on West's fearless style. Although only six-foot-three-inches and 185 pounds, West played like a giant. He battled among the giants: blocking shots, scrapping for rebounds, and jumping above the basket with his incredible leaping ability.

In 1972, years of frustration came to an end for West. The Lakers had reached the NBA finals seven times, only to lose each time. Finally, he won his long-sought NBA championship.

JERRY WEST

BORN: May 28, 1938, Cheylan, West Virginia.

HIGH SCHOOL: East Bank, WV.

COLLEGE: West Virginia University, Morgantown, WV, 1956–1960.

PRO: Los Angeles Lakers, 1961–1974.

RECORDS: Fifth highest career scoring average in basketball history; All-time leading scorer in play-off history.

HONORS: MVP, 1972.

West's unusually long arms helped him to snatch rebounds before his opponents could get to them.

Notes by Chapter

Rick Barry

1. Rudolph Wurlitzer, "Fastest Gun in the West," *The Saturday Evening Post* (March 11, 1967), pp. 80–82.
2. Tony Kornheiser, "Rick Barry," *Sports Illustrated* (April 25, 1983), pp. 84–96.
3. "Rick Barry," *Current Biography,* New York: The H.W. Wilson Company, 1971, pp. 25–27.
4. Wurlitzer, pp. 80–82.
5. Kornheiser, pp. 84–96.

Larry Bird

1. George Sullivan, "Larry Bird," *Great Lives: Sports* (New York: Charles Scribner's Sons), 1988 pp. 18–28.
2. Herbert Warren Wind, *The New Yorker* (March 24, 1986), pp. 54–84.
3. "Larry Bird," *Current Biography,* New York: The H.W. Wilson Company, 1982, pp. 34–37.
4. Jack McCallum, "Taken to the Limit," *Sports Illustrated* (May 30, 1988), p. 26.

Bob Cousy

1. Dave Anderson, "Final Whistle," *The Saturday Evening Post* (March 16, 1963), pp. 34–35.
2. Hal Butler, "Bob Cousy," *Sports Heroes Who Wouldn't Quit* (New York: Julian Messner), pp. 127-135.
3. "It's Easy for a 'Freak'," *Newsweek* (February 1, 1960), p. 55.
4. Mac Davis, "The Wizard Magician," *Basketball's Unforgettables,* (New York: Bantam, 1972), pp. 22–24.

Julius Erving

1. Jack Wilkinson, "Dr. J," *Atlanta Weekly* (April 5, 1987), pp. 8–11, 19, 22; Sam Goldaper, "The Legend of Dr. J Continues," *HOOP* (April 1993), pp. 54–56.
2. Mark Jacobson, "Doctor One and Only," *Esquire* (February 1985), pp. 112–119.

Magic Johnson

1. Magic Johnson, with Roy S. Johnson, "I'll Deal with It," *Sports Illustrated* (November 18, 1991), pp. 16–26.
2. "Earvin Johnson," *Current Biography,* New York: The H.W. Wilson Company, 1982, pp. 180–184.
3. Bruce Newman, "The Magic Man," *Sports Illustrated* (May 13, 1985), pp. 84–85, 89–96.
4. Ibid.

Michael Jordan

1. Jack McCallum, "The Desire Isn't There," *Sports Illustrated* (October 18, 1993), pp. 28–34.

2. Bill Gutman, "Michael Jordan," *Pro Sports Champions,* New York: Pocket Books—Archway Paperbacks, 1990, pp. 122–135.

3. Jack McCallum, "They're History," *Sports Illustrated* (June 28, 1993), pp. 17–21.

4. McCallum, "The Desire Isn't There," pp. 28–34.

George Mikan

1. "Mikan, the Marvel," *Newsweek* (April 2, 1945), p. 88.

2. George Mikan, "I Hope I Never Stop Growing," *The American Magazine* (December 30, 1953), pp. 30, 104–107.

3. Ibid.

4. Steve Jacobson, "Mikan Made This Game," *Newsday* (June 3, 1990), p. 8.

5. Ron Fimrite, "NBA Preview," *Sports Illustrated* (November 6, 1989), pp. 130–140.

Bob Pettit

1. "The Golden Hawk," *Time* (February 3, 1958), p. 62.

2. Bob Pettit with Stanley Frank, "Don't Call Us Freaks," *The Saturday Evening Post* (January 5, 1957), pp. 21, 64–66.

Oscar Robertson

1. "Oscar On the Loose," *Time* (January 20, 1958), p. 46.

2. Edward Linn, "There's No Telling How High He Can Go," *The Saturday Evening Post* (March 9, 1968), pp. 63–64.

Jerry West

1. Allen Camell: "Jerry West: The Perennial Mr. Clutch," *Basketball—Great Teams, Great Men, Great Moments* New York: Bantam, 1972, pp. 95–97.

2. John Underwood, "The Eye of an Eagle and a Big Wingspread," *Sports Illustrated* (February 8, 1965), pp. 14–17.

3. Ibid.

4. George Vecsey, "Jerry West, Greatest Clutch Player," *Pro Basketball Champions* (New York: Scholastic Book Series, 1970), pp. 24–37.

Index